Read for a
Better World™

GARBAGE COLLECTORS

A First Look

PERCY LEED

GRL Consultant, Diane Craig, Certified Literacy Specialist

Lerner Publications ◆ Minneapolis

Educator Toolbox

Reading books is a great way for kids to express what they're interested in. Before reading this title, ask the reader these questions:

> What do you think this book is about? Look at the cover for clues.

> What do you already know about garbage collectors?

> What do you want to learn about garbage collectors?

Let's Read Together

Encourage the reader to use the pictures to understand the text.

Point out when the reader successfully sounds out a word.

Praise the reader for recognizing sight words such as *is* and *an*.

TABLE OF CONTENTS

Garbage Collectors

Garbage collectors pick up trash.

Think Green,
Think Clean.
We run on clean burning natural gas.
wm.com
WM
WASTE MANAGEMENT
WM
WASTE MANAGEMENT
800 723 5060
SOLID WASTE
Join our team, we're hiring.
312438
McNeilus

These workers drive garbage trucks.

Some trucks have
an arm.
The arm lifts the bins.

bin
arm
DANGER
DANGER
9

Some trucks do
not have an arm.
The workers lift
the bins.

How are arms on
garbage trucks helpful?

11

Garbage collectors
work on streets.

They wear bright shirts.
The shirts help people
see them.

They wear gloves too.
This keeps their
hands safe.

How do gloves keep a
worker's hands safe?

15

Some garbage workers pick up trash in parks.

17

The truck is full.

18

The trash goes to a dump.

Garbage collectors work hard to keep places clean!

You Connect!

What is something you like about garbage collectors?

How can a garbage collector help you?

Would you like to be a garbage collector when you grow up?

Social and Emotional Snapshot

Student voice is crucial to building reader confidence. Ask the reader:

What is your favorite part of this book?

What is something you learned from this book?

Did this book remind you of any community helpers you've met?

Photo Glossary

Learn More

Earley, Ryan. *Garbage Trucks*. Coral Springs, FL: Seahorse Publishing, 2023.

Kaiser, Brianna. *All about Garbage Collectors*. Minneapolis: Lerner Publications, 2023.

Toolen, Avery. *A Day with a Garbage Collector*. Minneapolis: Jump!, 2022.

Index

Photo Acknowledgments

The images in this book are used with the permission of: © Andrey_Popov/Shutterstock Images, pp. 4–5; © EQRoy/Shutterstock Images, pp. 6–7, 23 (bottom left); © ImageegamI/iStockphoto, pp. 8–9, 23 (top left); © M2020/Shutterstock Images, pp. 10–11; © BrandonKleinPhoto/Shutterstock Images, p. 12; © Phovoir/Adobe Stock, p. 13; © hedgehog94/Shutterstock Images, pp. 14–15; © PeopleImages/iStockphoto, pp. 14, 23 (bottom right); © Julia Gomina/iStockphoto, pp. 16–17; © Christina Hemsley/Shutterstock Images, p. 16; © degetzica/Shutterstock Images, p. 18; © Dalibor Danilovic/Shutterstock Images, pp. 19, 23 (top right); © PeopleImages.com - Yuri A/Shutterstock Images, p. 20.

Cover Photograph: © Nadya So/iStockphoto

Design Elements: © Mighty Media, Inc.

Lerner Publications Company
An imprint of Lerner Publishing Group, Inc.
241 First Avenue North
Minneapolis, MN 55401 USA

For reading levels and more information, look up this title at www.lernerbooks.com.

Main body text set in Mikado a Medium.
Typeface provided by Hannes von Doehren.

Library of Congress Cataloging-in-Publication Data

Names: Leed, Percy, 1968–author.
Title: Garbage collectors : a first look / Percy Leed.
Description: Minneapolis, MN : Lerner Publications, [2025] | Series: Read about community helpers | Includes bibliographical references and index. | Audience: Ages 5–8 | Audience: Grades K–1 | Summary: "Young readers will love being able to ride along with garbage collectors in this fun text. Engaging photographs help learners understand where our trash goes and why these workers are so important to our communities"—Provided by publisher.
Identifiers: LCCN 2023035548 (print) | LCCN 2023035549 (ebook) | ISBN 9798765626429 (library binding) | ISBN 9798765629543 (paperback) | ISBN 9798765636848 (epub)
Subjects: LCSH: Refuse collectors—Juvenile literature. | Refuse collection—Juvenile literature.
Classification: LCC HD8039.R46 L44 2025 (print) | LCC HD8039.R46 (ebook) | DDC 628.4/42023–dc23/eng/20230802
LC record available at https://lccn.loc.gov/2023035548
LC ebook record available at https://lccn.loc.gov/2023035549

Manufactured in the United States of America
1 - CG - 7/15/24